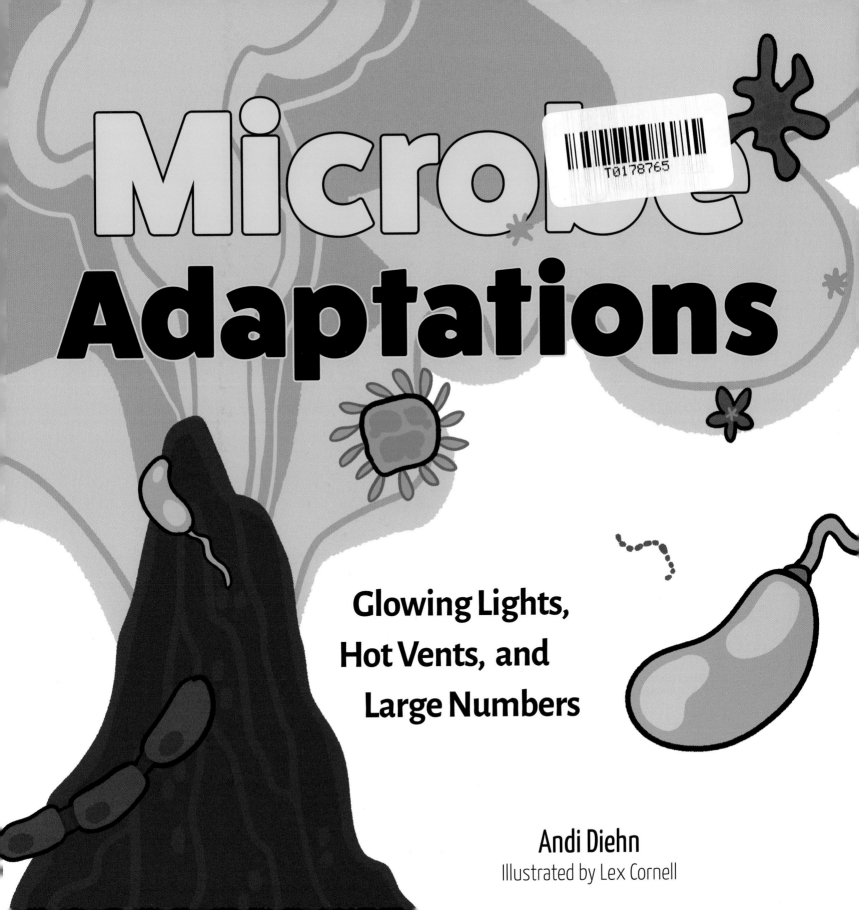

Microbe Adaptations

Glowing Lights, Hot Vents, and Large Numbers

Andi Diehn

Illustrated by Lex Cornell

EXPLORE MORE PICTURE BOOK ADAPTATIONS!

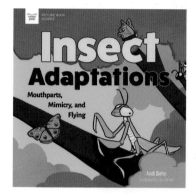

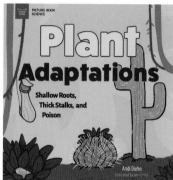

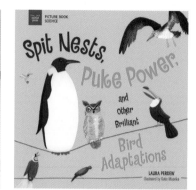

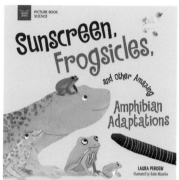

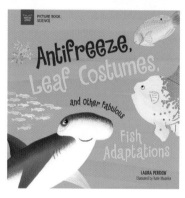

Check out more titles at www.nomadpress.net

Nomad Press

A division of Nomad Communications

10 9 8 7 6 5 4 3 2 1

This book was manufactured by
CGB Printers, North Mankato, Minnesota
November 2024, Job #1082660

ISBN Softcover: 978-1-64741-135-0
ISBN Hardcover: 978-1-64741-132-9

Educational Consultant, Marla Conn

Questions regarding the ordering of this book should be addressed to
Nomad Press
PO Box 1036, Norwich, VT 05055
www.nomadpress.net

Printed in the United States.

If you meet a microbe, you might want to make friends.
AFTER ALL, MICROBES KEEP US HEALTHY!

Or you might want to hide.
AFTER ALL, MICROBES CAN MAKE US SICK!

Or you might want to offer the microbe sunglasses.
BECAUSE SOME MICROBES GLOW SO BRIGHTLY!

Or you might want to make space in your freezer.
BECAUSE SOME MICROBES THRIVE IN THE COLD!

Or you might want to start counting.
BECAUSE MICROBES MULTIPLY REALLY FAST!

But whatever you do, be sure to thank the microbe.
BECAUSE WITHOUT MICROBES,
WE WOULDN'T EXIST!

Microbes are TEENY, TINY ORGANISMS.

Smaller than your
pinky nail.

Smaller than a
crumb.

In fact, about
a thousand microbes
could fit into the period
at the end of this sentence.

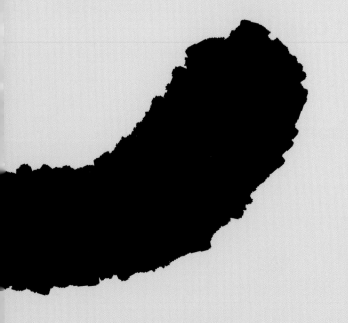

We can't see most of them without a **microscope,** but microbes are everywhere. They have **adapted** to live:

In the air,

in the dirt,

even in your body!

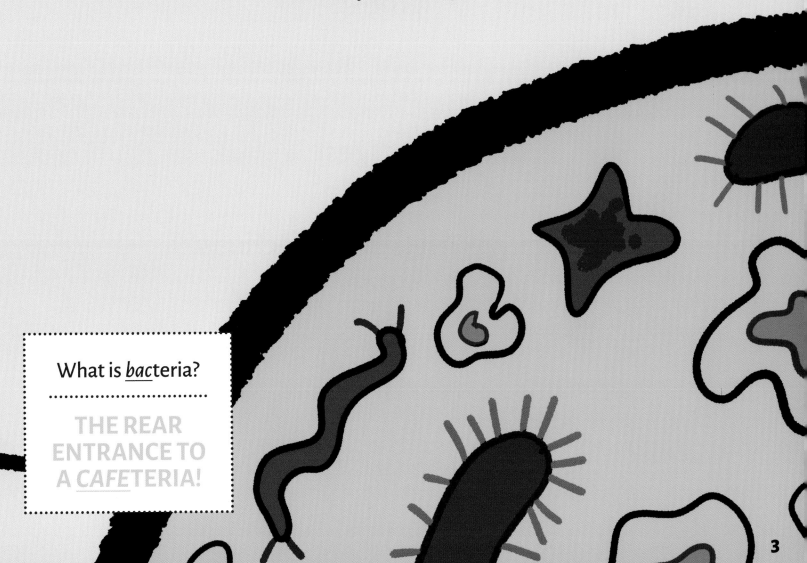

What is <u>bac</u>teria?

THE REAR
ENTRANCE TO
A <u>CAFE</u>TERIA!

3

There are five different kinds of microbes:

viruses,

bacteria,

archaea,

fungi, and

protists.

Some microbes are very helpful.
They help us **digest** our food.

They protect us from **infections**
that make us sick.

In fact, people can't survive without microbes!
We have adapted to live with microbes,
and they have adapted to live with us.

You know what else
can't live without microbes?

VIRUS

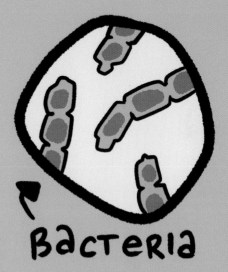

Bacteria

archaea

FUNGI

PROTIST

5

Anglerfish!

Anglerfish live
deep in the ocean.

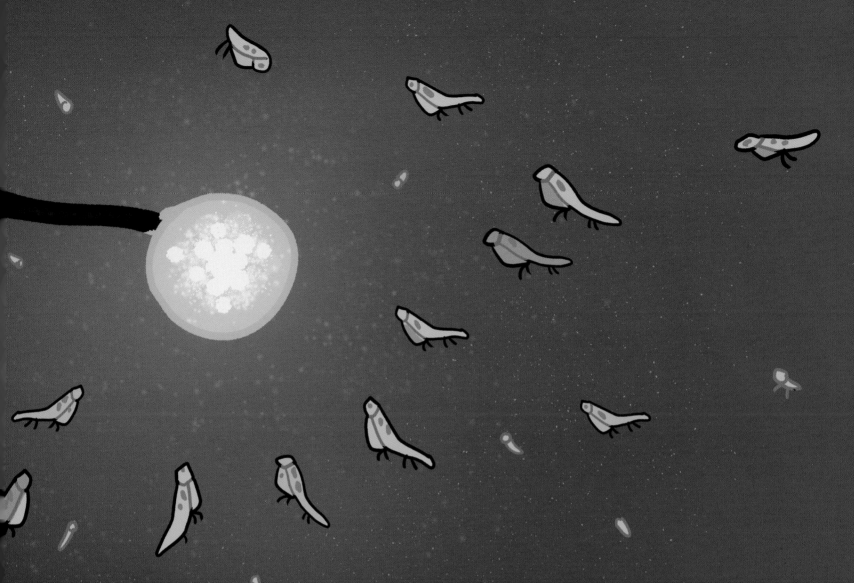

Female anglerfish are famous for the lights dangling from their foreheads. Plankton such as tiny fish, plants, and other animals are attracted to the light. They swim so close that all the anglerfish has to do is open its mouth and…

BREAKFAST IS SERVED!

But the anglerfish isn't
the one making the light.

Instead, this light is **bioluminescence**
from bacteria!

Bioluminescence is the ability to make light.

Some bacteria have **adapted** to the darkness of the deep ocean by having chemicals in their bodies that make light.

What type of flowers do bacteria like?

···

GERMANIUMS!

There's that word
again: **adapt.**

Adaptation is when
something changes so it fits
better in its environment.

This takes a loooong time.

How does it work?

Microbes with
traits that
help them survive
live long enough
to **reproduce** and pass
down these characteristics.
That means the microbes
with the right chemicals
for bioluminescence
make more microbes with
those same chemicals.

The bacteria that don't have the light-'em-up chemicals don't survive long enough to reproduce.

Eventually, bacteria that can glow are the only ones living on the angler fish. That species of bacteria has adapted.

Sometimes, a microbe cell makes a mistake, and that mistake becomes an adaptation.

Let's look at more microbe adaptations!

Some microbes
have adapted to live
in extremely hot
environments—such as
near the
hydrothermal vents
deep in the ocean!

These microbes are called
thermophiles.

THEY LOVE HEAT!

Scientists discovered these vents during the 1970s. Before that, people thought every living thing needed sunlight to live. But there's no sunlight that deep in the ocean.

Instead, vents in the ocean floor let out hot water mixed with chemicals.

And that's where some forms of life are thriving— including certain types of microbes.

What else can you find there?

Tubeworms!

Scaly-foot gastropods!

What do you call
a crab that never
shares its toys?
....
SHELLFISH!

Yeti crabs!

All of these organisms
have adapted to living
in extreme heat.

Thermophiles survive
best where it's hot-hot-hot
because their bodies contain
chemicals that keep them
from breaking down.

Some microbes **like it hot**, and some **like it super cold!**

Scientists have found microbes living on **glaciers**
where it's too cold for any other organisms
unless they are wrapped in coats, scarves, and hats!

These microbes are called
psychrophiles.

They live near or in
tiny cracks in the ice
that are filled with water.

These psychrophiles have adapted to the cold. They have chemicals in their bodies that keep them from freezing.

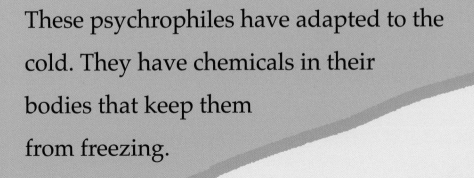

They can gain the **nutrients** they need from the water they find!

If you were on this glacier, you wouldn't really be able to see the psychrophiles—too small!

Let's look at some microbes closer to home—inside you!

Have you ever had an ear infection or a bad cough?
Some infections are caused by bacteria.

Maybe the doctor gave you a medicine called
an **antibiotic** to help you get better.
Antibiotics kill bacteria or stop them from reproducing.

Which runs faster, a hot or a cold?

·······················

A HOT,
BECAUSE
ANYONE
CAN CATCH
A COLD!

18

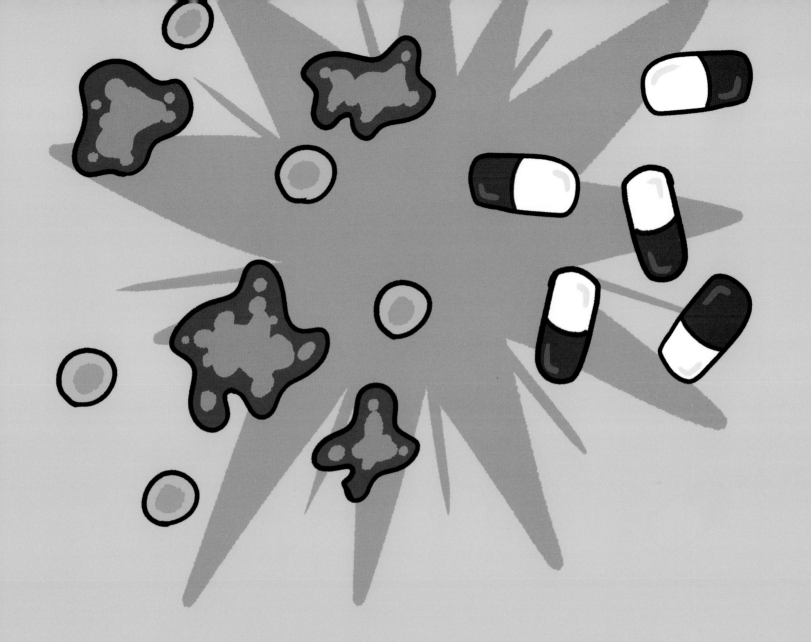

But . . . bacteria can fight back! They can adapt!

Bacteria can recognize antibiotics and avoid them.

Some bacteria pump the medicine away from them.
Others form chemicals to keep themselves
safe from the antibiotics.

The bacteria that survive the antibiotics are the ones that **reproduce** and create new bacteria.

And these new bacteria are also adapted to fight off the antibiotics.

Bacteria can reproduce super fast—sometimes in only a minute!

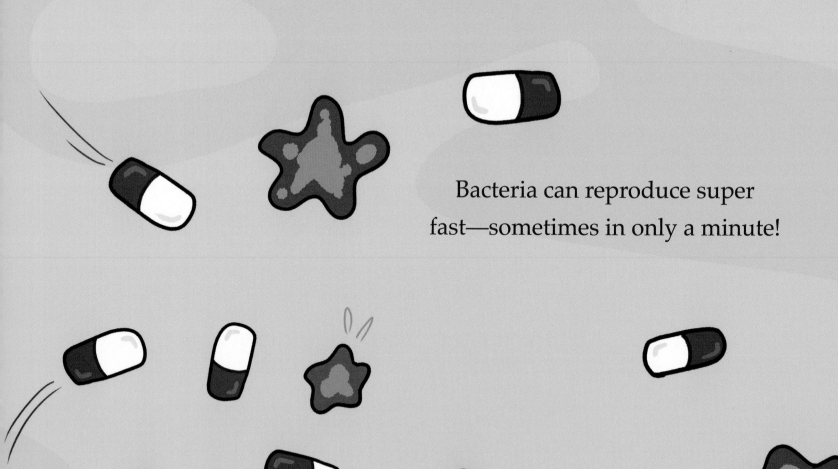

That means you can end up with a huge number of bacteria that fight off antibiotics.

Scientists work hard to find new medicines that bacteria haven't developed adaptations to dodge.

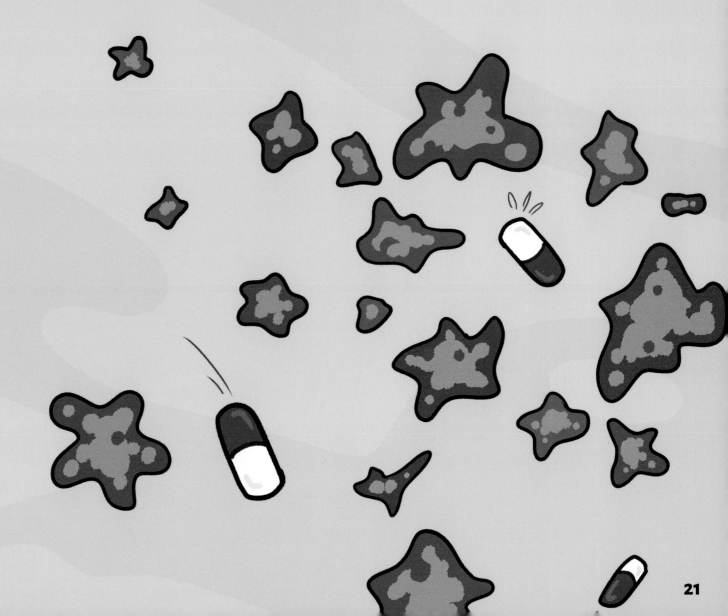

Hey! That's another adaptation!

Microbes can double in number in
as little as 20 minutes! That's a great
way for the species to survive.

Imagine suddenly having
thousands of new cousins!

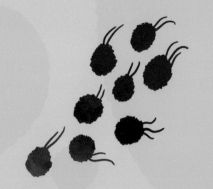

Why did the bacteria cross the microscope?

....

TO GET TO THE OTHER SLIDE!

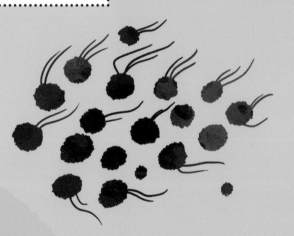

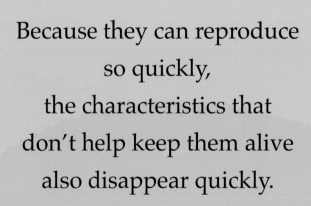

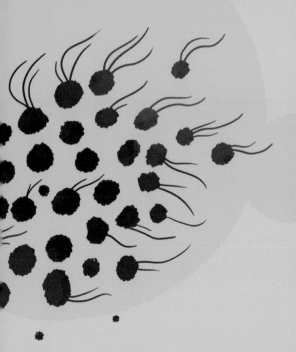

Because they can reproduce
so quickly,
the characteristics that
don't help keep them alive
also disappear quickly.

Let's look at one more
microbe adaptation.

Take a deep breath. What happens?

Your body gets oxygen!

Humans,
animals,
and plants
all need oxygen to live.

Some microbes are **anaerobic,** which means they live just fine in places without oxygen. Such as in your body—especially your gut!

Many of these anaerobic microbes help keep us alive. They work at digesting our food. They fight against bacteria that can make us sick. Humans have adapted to depend on the microbes inside our guts.

Microbes are **amazing at adapting** to their environment, all around the world. Maybe someday we'll even discover microbes that have adapted to living in space!

Microbes in Action!

What You Need

*a balloon - a glass bottle or jar -
warm water - yeast from the grocery store*

What You Do

- Fill the jar half full with warm water.

- Sprinkle a packet of yeast into the water.

- Fit the balloon over the mouth of the jar
  and set the jar aside for a few hours.

- What happens to the balloon? Yeast is a microbe.
  When the yeast mixes with the warm water, a
  chemical reaction takes place and carbon dioxide
  is released. That carbon dioxide rises through
  the jar, into the balloon, and blows it up!

Try It! Try the experiment with two jars. Put one on
the kitchen counter and one in the refrigerator. What
happens? What kind of adaptation might explain this?

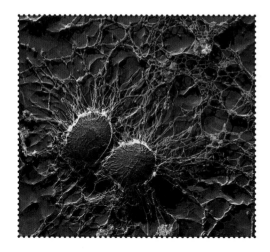

There are more microbes on Earth than there are any other lifeforms—by far!

Some microbes have a flagellum, which looks like a little tail and helps the microbe move.

Microbes were the first living organisms on the planet.

Bacteria can be different colors, and some bacteria can change color!

Scientists believe microbes could survive on Mars.

Microbes have been on the planet for at least 3.5 billion years. They are the oldest lifeform.

The Humongous Fungus is the largest living organism on Earth — it covers 2,400 acres!

There are more bacteria cells in your body than human cells.

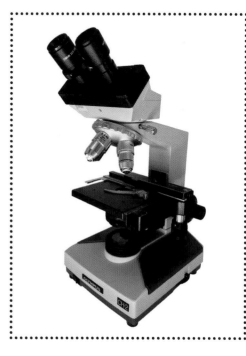

Glossary

adaptation: a change that a living thing makes to become better suited to its environment.

anaerobic: living without oxygen.

antibiotic: a medicine that destroys bacteria or stops them from growing.

bioluminescence: the ability of an organism to create light.

characteristic: a feature or quality.

chemical: an element that is a building block for everything in the world. Some chemicals can be combined or broken up to make different chemicals.

environment: the area in which something lives.

hydrothermal vent: a crack in the sea floor where very hot water comes out.

infection: illness caused by bacteria.

microbe: a tiny living or nonliving thing.

nutrient: a substance in food, soil, water, or air that living things need to live and grow.

organism: a living thing.

plankton: tiny organisms floating in the ocean.

psychrophile: a cold-loving organism.

reproduce: when animals and plants have offspring.

species: a group of plants or animals that are closely related and produce offspring.

thermophile: a heat-loving organism.

trait: a characteristic.

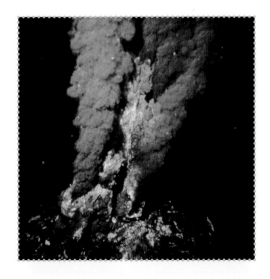

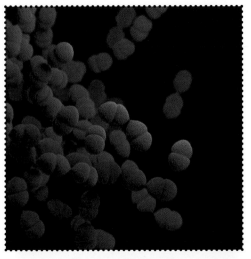